Is Bigfoot Real?

BY PATRICK PERISH

D1174739

amicus
high interest

Amicus High Interest is published by Amicus
P.O. Box 1329, Mankato, MN 56002
www.amicuspublishing.us

Library of Congress Cataloging-in-Publication Data
Perish, Patrick.
 Is bigfoot real? / by Patrick Perish.
    pages cm -- (Unexplained, what's the evidence?)
 Includes bibliographical references and index.
 Summary: "Presents the evidence (or lack therof) and stories
of both reported sightings and hoaxes of the large, hairy,
man-like creature known as Bigfoot or Sasquatch"-- Provided
by publisher.
 ISBN 978-1-60753-387-0 (library binding) -- ISBN 978-1-
60753-435-8 (ebook)
1. Sasquatch--Juvenile literature. I. Title.
 QL89.2.S2P475 2014
 001.944--dc23
                           2012048054

Editor   Rebecca Glaser
Series Designer   Kathleen Petelinsek
Page production   Red Line Editorial, Inc.

Photo Credits
Roberto A. Sanchez/Getty Images, cover; 123RF, 5;
Oldrich Hora/Dreamstime, 6; iStockphoto, 9; Antonio
Abrignani/123RF, 11; Iv Nikolny/Shutterstock Images, 12;
AP Images, 15, 22; Dreamstime, 16; iStockphoto/Thinkstock,
19; Sean Murray/123RF, 21; Chuck Stoody/AP Images, 25;
Nattawat Yenpech/123RF, 26; Russell Linton/Dreamstime, 29

Printed in the United States of America at Corporate Graphics
in North Mankato, Minnesota.
112013 / P.O. 1179
10 9 8 7 6 5 4 3 2

Table of Contents

What Is Bigfoot?

We don't always see animals in the woods. Bears, wolves, and big cats often stay hidden. But they are there. Maybe there is something else there, too. Stories tell of a giant hairy animal that walks on two feet. Is it a big ape? Is it human? Or does the animal called Bigfoot exist only in stories?

Some people think Bigfoot
lives in forests.

People all over the world have different names for Bigfoot.

 Q Who looks for Bigfoot?

Bigfoot is often seen in western Canada and the western United States. But stories of giant apes are told around the world. The animal has many names. In Asia, they call it a Yeti. Some call it the **Abominable** Snowman. Almas is its name in Mongolia. In Canada, they call it a Sasquatch. People search for it. But the furry beast is still a mystery.

 A person who looks for Bigfoot is called a **cryptozoologist**. It means a person who studies "hidden animals."

Stories of Bigfoot say he is tall. He is covered in hair like an ape and he stinks. He walks standing up like a human. Of course, his feet are big. His feet are said to be 1.5 to 2 feet (45 to 60 cm) long! Most Bigfoot hunters don't see the animal. Instead, they see mysterious tracks and hear strange sounds.

 How do Bigfoot hunters keep proof of tracks?

Did a Bigfoot leave these tracks in the snow?

Bigfoot hunters take pictures of tracks. Or they make a **cast** of them. They use plaster to keep the shape of the footprint.

First Reports

Many ancient stories tell of wild men. They look like humans covered in hair. In some stories, the wild man was human. He left his friends and family to live alone in the woods. He stopped wearing clothes and grew a thick coat of fur. The wild man protects animals and nature. Could these old stories have been based on real people or animals?

This "hairy man" was real. He lived in Asia in the 1800s.

Nepal is a rocky country. The **Sherpa** people live in the mountains. They have many stories of the Yeti. In some temples, they have holy pelts. A **pelt** is a piece of animal fur. The Sherpa legends say their pelts are from Yetis. Other people have said they are from bears or other animals.

The Sherpa people live in Nepal. Some claim to have seen a Yeti.

Bigfoot Stories

In 1951, explorers were in Nepal. They had come to climb Mount Everest. One day, Eric Shipton found strange tracks in the snow. They were bigger and wider than his boots. They had five toes. A Sherpa guide said they were Yeti tracks. Shipton took pictures. He followed the tracks. But he never saw the animal.

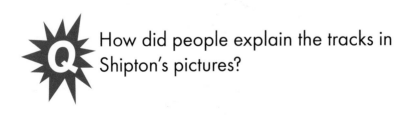 How did people explain the tracks in Shipton's pictures?

Eric Shipton and three others explored Mount Everest in 1951.

 Some said a smaller animal made them. High in the mountains, snow in small tracks can melt into huge footprints!

In 1967, Roger Patterson and his friend were riding horses in the woods. They were far from any roads. Suddenly, they saw a Bigfoot. Patterson filmed it. The Bigfoot looked at them and then walked away. Some think the video is a fake. But no one has been able to prove it.

Photos taken of Bigfoot have not proved that it is real.

Many others have tried to record Bigfoot. A 2009 video from Russia showed Bigfoot. It walked on top of a cliff. In 2010, a boy in Georgia saw Bigfoot near his home. He took a video. In the videos, Bigfoot has very long arms. It hides behind trees. But all the videos are blurry. It is hard to tell if they are real.

People sometimes say they see Bigfoot in the mountains.

Exposing the Fakes

A famous Bigfoot story happened in 1958. Workers were building a road in California. They found huge animal tracks around their bulldozers. They called the animal "Big Foot." The name stuck. In 2002, Ray Wallace died. He was one of the workers. His family said that he faked those tracks and many more.

 How did Ray Wallace fake the tracks?

This footprint is big!
But it is also fake.

 He used giant wooden shoes. He walked around the work site. He wanted to play a joke on the other workers.

21

In the 1960s, a Bigfoot body turned up. Frank Hansen showed it at fairs in a block of ice. He charged 35 cents per person to see his "Iceman." Experts thought the body could be real. But when they showed up to examine it, Hansen disappeared. So did the Iceman. A movie company later admitted it made the body for Hansen.

People wonder whether this is Bigfoot or someone dressed up.

Grover Krantz was a scientist in Washington. He studied Bigfoot. He said that Bigfoot tracks were impossible to fake. In 1990, a construction worker sent Krantz a cast. Krantz said it matched other Bigfoot tracks! Then, the construction worker revealed it was a fake. Even scientists can be fooled.

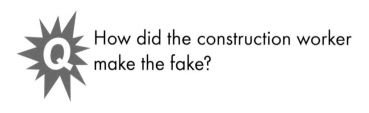 How did the construction worker make the fake?

Grover Krantz holds a footprint cast from a Bigfoot sighting.

 He used his cat's litter box. He filled it with mud. He molded the mud into a footprint. Then he took a cast of it.

Researchers have never found
Bigfoot bones or homes.

What's the Evidence?

Most scientists believe Bigfoot is not real. Why? There are no signs of it. No one has found Bigfoot bones or a Bigfoot body. There aren't any traces of homes or droppings. Scientists also think there would have to be a lot of Bigfoots—many more than reports tell about. They would need to **breed**. Otherwise they would go **extinct**.

Bigfoot may not be real. But he is famous! People in Willow Creek, California, hold a fair called Bigfoot Days every year. People have reported seeing Bigfoot near the town.

There is little **evidence** for Bigfoot. But year after year, stories come in. Will we find proof of Bigfoot someday?

Some places that have had many Bigfoot sightings post road signs!

BIG FOOT
XING

DUE TO SIGHTINGS
IN THE AREA OF A
CREATURE RESEMBLING
"BIG FOOT" THIS SIGN
HAS BEEN POSTED
FOR YOUR SAFETY

29

Glossary

abominable Awful or horrible.

breed To mate and produce young.

cast A plaster copy of something, such as a footprint.

cryptozoologist A person who studies "hidden" animals.

evidence Information, facts, or a visible sign that proves the truth of something.

extinct When an animal has completely died out and there are no more living.

pelt A piece of animal skin with fur still on it.

Sherpa A member of a group of people that live in the Himalayas and often serve as guides for mountain climbers.

Read More

Burgan, Michael. *The Unsolved Mystery of Bigfoot.* First Facts: Unexplained Mysteries. North Mankato, Minn.: Capstone Press, 2013.

Halls, Kelly Milner. *In Search of Sasquatch.* Boston: Houghton Mifflin, 2011.

Theisen, Paul. *Bigfoot.* Torque: The Unexplained. Minneapolis: Bellwether Media, 2011.

Worth, Bonnie. *Looking for Bigfoot.* Step into Reading. New York: Random House, 2010.

Websites

Bigfoot for Kids
http://www.squidoo.com/bigfoot-for-kids

The Evidence for Bigfoot
http://animal.discovery.com/tv-shows/finding-bigfoot/lists/bigfoot-evidence.htm

Index

About the Author

Patrick Perish spent many childhood nights under the covers with a flashlight and good book. In particular, aliens, ghosts, and other unexplained mysteries have always kept him up until the wee hours of the night. He lives in Minneapolis, MN where he writes and edits children's books.